HOW TO SEDUCE A WOMAN : SECRETS FOR SUCCESSFUL SEDUCTION

AURNY AIRDUVAL

HOW TO SEDUCE A WOMAN : SECRETS FOR SUCCESSFUL SEDUCTION

Foreword

Since my adolescence, I've always been intrigued and drawn to the art of seduction. The idea of understanding what makes people attractive and how to create a deep connection with someone has always fascinated me. Over the years, I've explored different approaches, read books, attended trainings, and most importantly, I've had the opportunity to experiment in the field.

It all started during my teenage years. Like many young people, I found myself facing my first romantic feelings and the uncertainties that come with them. I read magazines, listened to love songs, and watched romantic movies hoping to find clues to capture the attention of those I was interested in. That's how I discovered the initial concepts of seduction.

My first experiences with seduction were both exciting and sometimes puzzling. I understood that each person is unique, and there's no magic formula to seduce someone. I learned that authenticity and self-confidence are essential. My approaches evolved. I realised that active listening and empathy were just as important as seeking to charm.

My thirst to understand the art of seduction never waned. I read books on psychology, personal development, and writings of great seducers from the past. I studied nonverbal communication, social influence, and attraction. Each new discovery allowed me to refine my understanding of what works and what doesn't.

Of course, there were times when my attempts at seduction were unsuccessful, even clumsy. I learned through my mistakes and failures, taking a step back to understand what hadn't worked and how I could improve. However, I also experienced great successes that reinforced my belief that seduction is a subtle blend of art and science.

Throughout my journey, I realised that seduction is not manipulation or a game to get what one wants from others. On the contrary, it's an approach based on respect and mutual consent. I learned the importance of considering the feelings and desires of the other person and acting with integrity.

Over time, I discovered that seduction takes different forms depending on individuals and cultures. What may be seductive to one person may not be to another. Everyone has their own tastes and preferences, and there's no universal recipe. That's why it's essential to be open to the diversity of approaches and to adapt to each person's needs.

Through this book, I want to share with you the lessons from my journey in the art of seduction. My goal is to impart practical advice, based on experience, to help you develop your self-confidence, improve your communication skills, and create authentic connections with people you're attracted to. I believe that everyone can learn and grow in this area, and I hope this book will inspire and guide you to succeed in the art of seduction.

Chapter 1

Understanding the expectations and desires of women

To succeed in the art of seduction, it's essential to understand the expectations and desires of women. Each woman is unique and has specific needs, but there are nevertheless certain general tendencies that can help us better understand what they're looking for in a relationship. I'll share with you the insights I've gained from my experience and conversations with different women to help you better understand their expectations and desires.

1. The importance of active listening: one of women's fundamental expectations is to be listened to and understood. They appreciate men who are attentive to what they say, who ask relevant questions, and who show genuine interest in their feelings. Active listening is a powerful way to show that you care about them as individuals, not just as objects of seduction.

2. Sincerity and authenticity: Women are generally attracted to authentic men who show themselves as they are, without masks or pretense. Sincerity is a valuable quality that inspires trust and shows that

you're genuine in your intentions. Avoid artificial seduction strategies and be yourself, because it's when you're authentic that you create a real connection with a woman.

3. Self-confidence and assurance: Well-placed self-confidence is a real magnet for women. They're attracted to men who stand tall, who have a confident posture, and who exude self-assurance. However, it's important to distinguish self-confidence from arrogance. Be sure of yourself, but remain humble and respectful towards others.

4. Respect and attention to detail: Women appreciate men who are respectful towards them and towards others. Respect is a fundamental value in a relationship, and it's manifested in how you treat a woman, respond to her needs, and respect her choices and boundaries. Be considerate and attentive to the small details that matter to her, as they can make all the difference.

5. Emotional communication: Women attach great importance to emotional communication in a relationship. They want to share their feelings, emotions, and experiences with someone who understands and supports them. Learn to listen to her emotions, to welcome them without judgment, and to express yours with openness and vulnerability.

6. Humour and lightness: Humour is a powerful seduction tool. Women appreciate men who can make them laugh, who have a well-developed sense of humour, and who can bring lightness into the relationship. However, be careful not to use humour in

a hurtful or inappropriate way, and respect everyone's boundaries.

7. Taking initiative: While women appreciate caring and attentive men, they also value taking initiative. Show yourself determined and ready to act when necessary. It can be as simple as suggesting an outing, planning an activity together, or making decisions within the relationship.

By understanding these expectations and desires of women, you'll be better equipped to develop fulfilling and respectful relationships. Keep in mind that each woman is unique, and you'll need to adapt your approaches according to the person you want to seduce. The key to success lies in sincerity, authenticity, and understanding each other's needs.

Chapter 2

Developing self-confidence and self-esteem

Building Self-Confidence and Self-Esteem are key elements of successful seduction. By developing a strong belief in yourself and appreciating yourself for who you are, you'll feel more comfortable in your interactions with women and naturally attract their attention. I'll share practical tips with you for cultivating self-confidence and strengthening your self-esteem.

1. Identify your strengths and qualities: The first step in building self-confidence is becoming aware of your strengths and qualities. Make a list of your past achievements, skills, and talents. Also, consider your positive personality traits. By recognising what you have to offer, you'll feel more self-assured and able to value your uniqueness.

2. Overcome doubts and negative thoughts: It's normal to experience doubts and negative thoughts about yourself from time to time. However, it's essential not to let these thoughts define you. Learn to identify negative thinking patterns and replace them

with positive affirmations. Repeat encouraging messages to yourself every day to strengthen your self-esteem.

3. Set achievable goals: Having clear and achievable goals can give you a sense of direction and motivation. Whether it's in your personal, professional, or relational life, set specific and attainable goals. Every time you achieve a goal, you'll boost your self-confidence and self-esteem.

4. Step out of your comfort zone: Taking risks and stepping out of your comfort zone is an excellent way to develop self-confidence. Try new activities, socialise, and dare to face your fears. Each experience will help you grow and gain confidence.

5. Take care of yourself: Taking care of your physical, emotional, and mental well-being is essential for building self-confidence. Exercise regularly, eat healthily, get enough sleep, and engage in activities that relax and please you. The better you feel about yourself, the more your self-esteem will improve.

6. Surround yourself with positive people: Your environment plays a crucial role in building self-confidence. Surround yourself with positive, supportive, and encouraging people. Avoid those who criticise or belittle you, as they can negatively affect your self-esteem.

7. Learn from failures and mistakes: Failures and mistakes are part of life. Instead of seeing them as failures, view them as learning opportunities. Analyse

what didn't work and use that experience to grow and improve.

By developing self-confidence and self-esteem, you'll be better equipped to approach women with assurance and authenticity. Seduction begins with self-love and confidence in your abilities. Continue working on yourself and surrounding yourself with positivity to become an irresistible seducer.

Chapter 3

Developing an attractive and positive lifestyle

Developing an attractive and positive lifestyle is a key essential for successfully seducing women. By cultivating a fulfilling lifestyle, you'll naturally attract attention and pique the interest of women. I'll share tips with you for developing a lifestyle that allows you to radiate and draw women towards you.

1. Identify your passions and interests: an attractive life begins with pursuing your passions and interests. Take the time to identify what truly excites you and make these activities a priority in your life. Whether it's sports, music, art, travel, or any other activity that ignites your passion, sharing your passions with others emits a positive and attractive aura.

2. Adopt a positive attitude: a positive attitude is contagious and draws people towards you. Be optimistic and open-minded. Seek the bright side of things and avoid getting caught up in negativity. Women will be drawn to your positive energy and your ability to see the best in every situation.

3. Take care of your health and appearance: taking care of your physical health and appearance is an important way to attract women. Exercise regularly to feel good in your body and boost your confidence. Pay attention to your personal hygiene and dress style to present the best version of yourself.

4. Explore new experiences: an attractive lifestyle is characterized by curiosity and openness to new experiences. Try new activities, explore new places, meet new people. This openness to the unknown will broaden your horizons and make your life more interesting and captivating.

5. Surround yourself with positive people: as mentioned in the previous chapter, your circle plays a crucial role in your life. Surround yourself with positive people who support and inspire you. Friends who share your values and vision of life will help you maintain a fulfilling lifestyle.

6. Develop your social skills: developing an attractive lifestyle involves having good social skills. Learn to be comfortable in social situations, to listen attentively, to express your ideas confidently, and to build meaningful connections with others. These social skills will enable you to forge authentic relationships with women.

7. Stay authentic: the most important aspect of developing an attractive lifestyle is to remain authentic. Be yourself and don't try to impress or please at all costs. Women will be drawn to your true personality and sincerity.

By cultivating an attractive and positive lifestyle, you'll become a magnetic and appealing man. Women will naturally be attracted to your positive energy, self-confidence, and authenticity.

Chapter 4

Mastering the art of verbal communication

Mastering the art of verbal communication is a vital element of successful seduction. It is through speech that you express your ideas, emotions, and intentions. We'll explore verbal communication techniques that will enable you to connect authentically and deeply with the women you're seducing.

1. Active listening: effective communication starts with active listening. Be attentive when speaking to a woman. Listen to what she says, show interest in her stories and opinions. Ask questions to deepen the conversation and demonstrate that you're genuinely engaged in the exchange. Active listening will help you better understand the woman you're seducing and create a stronger bond with her.

2. Be clear and concise: clarity and conciseness are important qualities in verbal communication. Express your thoughts clearly and avoid getting lost in lengthy speeches. Women appreciate men who get straight to the point and can articulate themselves precisely.

3. Use body language: verbal communication isn't limited to words. Your body language plays a crucial role in seduction. Use open and confident gestures, maintain eye contact, and smile. Your body language sends powerful signals about your confidence and interest, strengthening your appeal in the eyes of women.

4. Avoid sensitive topics: when seducing a woman, it's best to avoid sensitive or controversial topics, at least in the early stages of the relationship. Keep the conversation light and positive. Avoid discussing political, religious, or any other potentially sensitive issues that could create tension.

5. Use humour: humour is a powerful tool for creating a connection with a woman. Use humour to lighten the mood, make your conversation partner laugh, and evoke positive emotions. Women love men who have a sense of humour and can make them laugh.

6. Express your emotions: don't be afraid to express your emotions sincerely and authentically. Share your feelings with the woman you're seducing and show her that you're open to vulnerability. Women appreciate men who can emotionally connect and are comfortable expressing their feelings.

7. Know when to listen and when to speak: successful communication involves knowing when to listen and when to speak. Pay attention to the verbal and non-verbal cues of the woman you're seducing. If she's talking a lot, take the time to listen and show interest in what she's saying. If she's more reserved,

take the initiative to lead the conversation gently and respectfully.

By mastering the art of verbal communication, you'll develop a deeper connection with the women you're seducing. Communication is the foundation of human relationships, and by using these techniques, you'll be able to create authentic and meaningful connections with the women you desire.

Chapter 5

Utilising nonverbal communication to your advantage

Nonverbal communication plays a fundamental role in seduction. It is through your gestures, posture, gaze, and facial expressions that you convey essential information about yourself and your intentions. We'll explore the various ways to use nonverbal communication to your advantage when seducing a woman.

1. Body language: your body language often speaks louder than your words. A straight and open posture demonstrates your confidence, while a closed-off posture may indicate insecurity. Be mindful of your body language and ensure you adopt an open, relaxed, and confident posture when in the presence of a woman you're seducing.

2. Eye contact: eye contact is a powerful weapon in seduction. Maintaining strong eye contact with the woman you desire shows your interest and confidence. However, avoid staring intensely or looking too insistently, as this could be misinterpreted as intruding into personal space.

3. Smiling: smiling is one of the simplest and most effective ways to create a connection with a woman. A warm and sincere smile projects a positive and friendly image of yourself. It also puts women at ease and builds trust.

4. Gestures: your gestures can reinforce your words and add life to the conversation. Use natural and expressive gestures to complement your speech. Avoid overly aggressive or nervous gestures, as they might be perceived as a sign of nervousness or insecurity.

5. Intonation: the intonation of your voice is also important in nonverbal communication. Speak in a calm, steady voice with pleasant intonation. Avoid speaking too quickly or murmuring, as this might give the impression that you lack confidence.

6. Physical proximity: physical proximity is another aspect of nonverbal communication to consider. Respect the personal space of the woman you're seducing and read her signals to know if she's comfortable with closer proximity. If she's receptive to physical closeness, it could be a sign that she's interested.

7. Facial expression: your facial expression can speak volumes about your emotions and state of mind. Try to maintain an open, relaxed, and friendly expression. Avoid fixed or closed expressions, as they could be interpreted as indifference or disinterest.

By using nonverbal communication intentionally and positively, you can enhance your appeal to the women you're seducing. Strong and consistent nonverbal communication reinforces the message you want to convey and allows you to create a deeper connection with the person you desire.

Chapter 6

Creating a memorable first impression

The first impression you make on a woman is crucial in the seduction process. It can determine whether she will be open to getting to know you further or if she will remain defensive. Let's explore how to create a memorable first impression that sparks interest and attraction in a woman.

1. Pay attention to your appearance: appearance plays an important role in the first impression you leave. Take the time to groom yourself before meeting a woman. Dress appropriately for the occasion and ensure you are well-groomed and clean. A neat appearance demonstrates your respect for yourself and others.

2. Show confidence, but not arrogance: confidence is attractive, but arrogance can be off-putting. Show yourself to be self-assured, but avoid coming across as pretentious or condescending. Display confidence in your gestures and words, but remain humble and open to interaction.

3. Practice active listening: when meeting a woman for the first time, actively listen to what she has to say. Ask relevant questions and show genuine interest in what she shares with you. Active listening is a sign of respect and empathy, qualities appreciated in any relationship.

4. Smile and be friendly: a warm and friendly smile is the simplest way to create a positive atmosphere during your first encounter. A sincere smile invites conversation and shows that you are open to establishing a connection.

5. Be authentic: authenticity is essential for creating a memorable first impression. Don't try to be someone you're not to please a woman. Stay true to yourself and show yourself as you truly are. An authentic person is more attractive because they exude genuine self-confidence.

6. Show your interest: make the woman you're seducing feel special by showing genuine interest in her. Ask her questions about her passions, interests, and life, and listen carefully to her responses. Show her that you sincerely care about who she is as a person.

7. Avoid controversial topics: during a first meeting, it's best to avoid controversial topics that could lead to debates or disagreements. Stick to light and positive subjects that foster a pleasant and relaxed atmosphere.

By creating a memorable first impression based on authenticity, active listening, and self-confidence, you can establish a positive connection with a woman from the very first moment. A successful first impression paves the way for deeper and more meaningful future exchanges.

Chapter 7

Flirting with subtlety and elegance

Flirting is a subtle art that allows one to express interest and attraction towards a woman in an elegant and non-intrusive manner. We will explore different flirting techniques that will enable you to charm a woman while remaining respectful and attentive.

1. Use body language: body language is a powerful way to communicate your interest without having to say a word. Use eye contact to establish a connection with the woman you're flirting with. A soft, sustained gaze can convey a lot about your feelings. Smile and tilt your head slightly to show that you're attentive to what she's saying.

2. Compliment sincerely: compliments are an effective way to flirt, but they should be sincere and not overdone. Choose compliments that highlight specific aspects of her personality, appearance, or achievements. Avoid overly generic compliments that may come across as insincere.

3. Use humour: humour is an excellent way to create a relaxed atmosphere and show your fun side. Display

wit and intelligence in your humorous remarks. However, avoid jokes that are too vulgar or offensive, as they may be misinterpreted.

4. Play with words: playing with words and double entendres can be a playful way to flirt subtly. Use phrases or expressions that can have a double meaning to create a conspiratorial bond with the woman you're flirting with.

5. Be attentive and listen: flirting involves being attentive to the needs and preferences of the woman you're seducing. Show her that you care about her by asking her questions about her tastes, passions, and interests. Listen carefully to her responses to demonstrate that you're genuinely interested in what she has to say.

6. Create moments of intimacy: look for opportunities to create moments of intimacy with the woman you're seducing. A one-on-one conversation in a quiet place or a tender gesture, like holding her hand delicately, can strengthen the emotional bond between you.

7. Know how to read signals: it's important to be able to read the signals a woman sends to determine if she's receptive to your flirting. If she seems comfortable, smiles, and engages in conversation positively, it may be a sign that she's interested. However, be attentive to any signs of discomfort or disinterest, and adjust your approach accordingly.

Flirting with subtlety and elegance is a way to show your interest and attraction while respecting the boundaries of the other person. By using body language, sincere compliments, humour, and attentive listening, you can create a deep connection with a woman and lay the groundwork for a fulfilling relationship.

Chapter 8

Understanding signals of interest and disinterest

When seducing a woman, it's essential to be able to recognize the signals she sends to determine if she's interested or not. Understanding these signals will allow you to adjust your approach and know whether it's appropriate to continue flirting or if it's better to take a step back. We'll look at the various signals of interest and disinterest that women may emit, so you can be more comfortable in your interactions.

1. Signals of interest: there are several signs that indicate a woman is interested in you and receptive to your flirtation. Here are some of these signals:

a. Eye contact: if a woman frequently looks you in the eyes and maintains eye contact, it's generally a sign of interest.

b. Smile: a warm and sincere smile is an obvious sign of interest and openness.

c. Body language: if she leans towards you, turns towards you, or adopts an open posture, it may indicate she is comfortable in your presence.

d. Attentive listening: if she asks you questions about yourself, shows interest in your passions and interests, it's a sign she's keen to learn more about you.

e. Compliments: if she compliments you on your appearance, talents, or achievements, it's a sign she enjoys your company.

2. Signals of disinterest: similarly, it's important to recognize signs that a woman is not interested in your advances. Here are some of these signals:

a. Lack of eye contact: if she avoids eye contact or looks elsewhere while you're talking, it could be a sign of disinterest.

b. Closed body language: if she crosses her arms, leans back, or adopts a closed posture, it may indicate she's uncomfortable or unreceptive.

c. Lack of engagement in conversation: if she appears distant, uninterested, or responds briefly, it could be a sign she's not interested in deepening the conversation.

d. Excuses to end the conversation: if she makes excuses to step away or end the conversation, it may be a sign she prefers not to prolong the interaction.

3. Knowing when to proceed and when to step back: it's important to know when to continue flirting and when to take a step back to respect the feelings and boundaries of the other person. If you perceive signals

of interest, feel free to continue the conversation and deepen your connection. However, if you notice signs of disinterest, it's best to take a step back and not insist. Respect her space and choices.

4. Being attentive to her reactions: it's essential to be attentive to her reactions and responses throughout the interaction. Pay attention to her verbal and non-verbal cues to understand her emotions and feelings. Remember that each woman is unique, and her signals may vary depending on her personality and experiences.

By understanding signals of interest and disinterest, you'll be able to navigate the seduction process more smoothly. Keep in mind that mutual respect and open communication are essential for building a sincere and fulfilling connection with a woman.

Chapter 9

Building an authentic emotional connection

When it comes to seducing a woman and building a lasting relationship, creating an authentic emotional connection is essential. Emotions play a key role in any meaningful relationship, as they allow individuals to understand, support, and share intense moments with each other. We will see how to create a strong and sincere emotional connection with a woman you are seducing.

1. Actively listening and showing empathy: Successful emotional communication begins with active listening and empathy. When talking to a woman, show interest in what she has to say and be attentive to her emotions. Ask open-ended questions to deepen your understanding of her feelings and thoughts. Express empathy by acknowledging her emotions and showing that you understand how she feels.

2. Sharing your emotions authentically: To create an emotional connection, it is important to share your own emotions authentically. Be open and honest about what you feel and express yourself sincerely. Share your

joys, sorrows, dreams, and aspirations. By being vulnerable and showing your true self, you allow the woman to know you on a deeper level and feel closer to you emotionally.

3. Demonstrating empathy and understanding: Empathy and understanding are essential for creating an authentic emotional connection. Put yourself in the other person's shoes and try to understand their experiences and feelings. Show them that you care about what they are going through and that you are there to support them. Practice patience and compassion in your interactions.

4. Creating moments of emotional intimacy: Moments of emotional intimacy are privileged times when you share deep and sincere emotions with the other person. This can be done through intimate conversations, tender gestures, or moments of sharing your deepest thoughts. These moments strengthen the emotional connection and create emotional intimacy that is essential for a fulfilling relationship.

5. Providing support and encouragement: Supporting and encouraging the other person in their projects, dreams, and aspirations strengthens the emotional connection. Be their greatest support, be there in difficult times, and celebrate their successes. When they know they can count on you for support and encouragement, the relationship becomes stronger and deeper.

6. Being present and attentive: Presence and attention are important aspects of emotional

connection. Be present in your interactions, put your phone aside, and give them your full attention. Show them that they are a priority for you and that you are emotionally invested in the relationship.

By creating an authentic emotional connection with the woman you are seducing, you establish the foundations of a strong and fulfilling relationship. When emotions are shared sincerely and empathy and support are present, the relationship strengthens and becomes more meaningful for both partners.

Chapter 10

Listening and showing empathy

Listening and showing empathy are among the most valuable skills in the art of seduction. Being an attentive listener helps create a deeper connection with the woman you're seducing, while empathy allows you to understand her emotions and thoughts more meaningfully.

1. Practice active listening: active listening is a key skill for establishing an emotional connection with the other person. When you're in conversation, fully concentrate on what she's saying without getting distracted. Ask questions to deepen your understanding and be receptive to her words. Show her that you genuinely care about what she's expressing.

2. Be open-minded: open-mindedness is essential for understanding different perspectives and experiences. Be willing to listen to her opinions, even if they differ from yours. Avoid making hasty judgments and show curiosity to learn more about what she thinks and feels.

3. Pay attention to non-verbal cues: when listening to a woman, pay attention to her non-verbal cues.

Facial expressions, body language, and gestures can reveal a lot about her emotions and feelings. Show her that you notice and understand these cues, which strengthens the emotional bond between you.

4. Validate her emotions: empathy also involves validating the other person's emotions. If she expresses feelings, don't minimize or ignore them. Instead, acknowledge her emotions and show her that you understand how she feels. This helps her feel heard and understood.

5. Avoid distractions: when you're with the woman you're seducing, steer clear of unnecessary distractions. Put away your phone or any other device that might divert your attention from the conversation. Show her that you're fully present and engaged in the exchange.

6. Exercise patience and respect: empathy also entails being patient and respectful towards the other person. Don't rush her for answers or information. Give her the necessary time to express her thoughts and emotions, and refrain from judging her. Show her that you respect her as a unique individual.

Being a good listener and showing empathy are essential qualities for establishing a deep emotional connection with a woman. These skills enable you to understand, support, and create a relationship based on trust and authenticity.

Chapter 11

Managing fears and rejections with confidence

When engaging in the art of seduction, it's inevitable to encounter fears and rejections. However, how you manage these emotions can make all the difference in your success in seduction. Let's explore strategies to overcome your fears and approach rejections with confidence.

1. Facing the fear of rejection: fear of rejection is one of the most common emotions in the seduction process. It's natural to fear being rejected by the woman you're trying to seduce. To overcome this fear, remind yourself that rejection is an integral part of seduction and doesn't necessarily reflect your worth as an individual. Learn not to take rejections personally and see each experience as an opportunity for learning and growth.

2. Boosting your self-confidence: self-confidence is essential for facing fears and rejections with assurance. Work on improving your self-esteem and recognizing your qualities and strengths. The more confident you are, the less impact rejections will have on your self-worth.

3. Learning from each experience: every interaction and rejection can be valuable learning opportunities. Take the time to reflect on your experiences and draw lessons from them. Ask yourself what you could have done differently or what you've learned about yourself. This reflection will help you grow and improve your seduction skills.

4. Maintaining a positive attitude: a positive attitude is crucial for facing seduction challenges with confidence. Develop an optimistic and realistic mindset, focusing on your progress and achievements rather than your failures. A positive attitude will help you overcome obstacles and maintain your motivation to continue progressing in your seduction journey.

5. Not fearing rejection: to succeed in the art of seduction, it's important not to fear rejection. Accept that rejection is part of the process and use it as an opportunity for self-improvement. The more comfortable you are with rejection, the more you'll be able to open yourself to new seduction opportunities.

6. Knowing when to persist and when to let go: it's essential to know when to persist in your advances and when to let go. Sometimes, it can be beneficial to keep trying to seduce a woman, especially if you feel there's potential for a deeper connection. However, it's also important to recognize when it's best to move on. Exercising discernment in these situations will allow you to manage fears and rejections with wisdom and assurance.

Managing fears and rejections with confidence is a key element to succeed in the art of seduction. By adopting a positive attitude, learning from each experience, and displaying self-confidence, you'll be better prepared to face the challenges that come your way. Keep in mind that a resilient and determined attitude will help you progress and develop your seduction skills while strengthening your self-confidence.

Chapter 12

Using humour and charm to seduce

Using humor and charm are two powerful tools in the seduction arsenal. They can help you establish an instant connection with a woman and make her laugh, which is a fantastic way to break the ice and put her at ease. Let's explore how to effectively use humor and charm to seduce and create a positive and enjoyable atmosphere.

1. The importance of humor in seduction: humor is an essential element of seduction. A well-developed sense of humor can help you relax the atmosphere, create a rapport with a woman, and make her feel comfortable in your presence. Humor can also be a subtle way to flirt and show your interest without being too direct.

2. Find your humor style: everyone has their own style of humor, and it's essential to find yours so that it's authentic and natural. Some people are naturally inclined towards light and teasing humor, while others prefer sarcastic or more subtle humor. Explore different humor styles and find the one that best suits your personality and that of the woman you're seducing.

3. Display charm and elegance: charm and elegance are also important assets in seduction. Develop a charismatic presence by listening to the other person, showing attention, and demonstrating genuine interest in what she says. Use your body language to show your confidence and sincere interest.

4. The art of teasing: teasing is a form of subtle humor that can be very effective in seduction. This involves making slightly teasing or mocking remarks to the person you're seducing. However, it's important to be tactful and not go too far to avoid hurting or offending.

5. Laughing together: laughter creates an emotional connection between people. Look for humor topics that you can share together, such as funny anecdotes or amusing jokes. Laughing together will strengthen the bond between you and make the seduction experience more enjoyable and memorable.

6. The importance of sincerity: humor and charm are more effective when you are authentic and sincere. Don't force a humor style that doesn't suit you or try to be someone you're not. Be yourself, be natural, and let your personality shine through the humor and charm you use in your seduction.

By using humor and charm authentically and kindly, you can establish an instant connection with a woman and seduce her in a subtle and enjoyable way. Keep in mind that humor is a powerful tool but must be used sensitively and with respect for the other person. With practice and confidence in yourself, you'll find that humor and charm can play a key role in the success of your seduction efforts.

Chapter 13

Establishing healthy and respectful boundaries

In any relationship, including within the context of seduction, establishing healthy and respectful boundaries is essential for maintaining a harmonious and fulfilling connection. We will explore the importance of setting clear boundaries, both for yourself and for your potential partner, in order to maintain a balanced and respectful dynamic.

1. Understanding your own boundaries: before you can set boundaries with someone else, it is crucial to understand your own boundaries and what you are willing to accept or not accept in a relationship. Reflect on your values, emotional needs, and desires, and be honest with yourself about what you are looking for in a relationship. This will enable you to define boundaries that suit you and communicate them clearly to your potential partner.

2. Expressing your boundaries with respect: once you have identified your boundaries, it is important to express them respectfully to your potential partner. Open and honest communication is key to establishing healthy boundaries. Be clear and precise in your

communication, without judgment or accusation. Make sure to communicate your boundaries calmly and understandingly, explaining why they are important to you.

3. Respecting the boundaries of the other person: just as you expect your own boundaries to be respected, it is essential to also respect the boundaries of your potential partner. Listen carefully to what they express and make sure not to cross their boundaries. Mutual respect for boundaries strengthens trust and mutual understanding in a relationship.

4. Establishing emotional boundaries: in addition to physical boundaries, it is equally crucial to establish emotional boundaries. This means taking the time to get to know the other person gradually, without rushing into emotional intimacy too quickly. Respect your potential partner's pace and give them the space they need to open up to you at their own pace.

5. The benefits of healthy boundaries: establishing healthy and respectful boundaries in seduction has many benefits. It shows that you respect yourself and also value the respect of the other person. Clear boundaries help establish a solid foundation for a healthy and balanced relationship, where the needs and desires of both partners are considered.

6. The role of ongoing communication: ongoing communication is essential for maintaining healthy boundaries throughout the relationship. Continue to talk about your feelings, needs, and boundaries as the relationship evolves. Boundaries may change over

time, and it is important to ensure that you and your partner are always on the same page.

By establishing healthy and respectful boundaries in seduction, you create an environment of trust and mutual understanding, thereby fostering the development of a deeper and more meaningful connection with your potential partner. When boundaries are clear and respected on both sides, the relationship has every chance to flourish and grow in a positive and harmonious dynamic.

Chapter 14

Demonstrating gallantry and courtesy

In the process of seduction, gallantry and courtesy play a crucial role in establishing an authentic and respectful connection with a woman. We'll explore the importance of these qualities and how to manifest them sincerely and naturally.

1. Modern gallantry: gallantry has evolved over time, but its essence remains essential in seduction. It involves being attentive to a woman, showing her respect and consideration. This can be demonstrated through small gestures like holding the door, offering assistance, or giving a small gift, always in a disinterested and respectful manner.

2. The importance of courtesy: courtesy is a sign of respect towards the other person and shows that you are attentive to their well-being. Be polite in your words and actions, listen attentively, and avoid any form of vulgar or disrespectful language. Courtesy shows that you value the feelings and needs of the other person.

3. Authenticity in gallantry: gallantry should not be a façade but rather an authentic manifestation of who you

are as a man. Be sincere in your gestures and words, without seeking to play a role. Authentic gallantry creates a lasting impression and shows your true personality.

4. Being attentive and sensitive: gallantry and courtesy also involve being attentive to the needs and preferences of the woman you are seducing. Be sensitive to what she expresses and adapt your actions accordingly. This shows that you care about her as a unique individual.

5. Avoiding stereotypes: be aware of gender stereotypes and avoid reproducing them in your interactions. Do not consider a woman as inferior or less capable, but rather treat her as an equal and potential partner. Respect her choices and opinions, even if they differ from yours.

6. The benefits of gallantry: gallantry and courtesy create an atmosphere of trust and mutual respect. These qualities strengthen the emotional bond with your potential partner and can evoke a sense of security and comfort. Authentic gallantry demonstrates your attention and sincere interest in her, and this can be a determining factor in the development of a fulfilling relationship.

Gallantry and courtesy are essential elements for successful seduction and a fulfilling relationship with a woman. Be authentic, attentive, and respectful in your interactions, and you will create a meaningful and lasting bond based on trust and mutual respect. Modern gallantry is a way to show your best self as a man, and

it will not go unnoticed by a woman who appreciates
the qualities of a true gentleman.

Chapter 15

Overcoming obstacles related to age difference

In a relationship where there is a significant age difference between partners, there can be specific obstacles to overcome. We will explore these challenges and offer strategies to address them constructively and fulfillingly.

1. Social perception: one of the primary difficulties couples with an age difference may encounter is societal perception and external judgments. Friends, family, and society may express negative opinions or concerns about this difference. It's important to remain confident in your relationship and not let others' stereotypes and prejudices affect you. Ensure that your relationship is based on a genuine emotional connection and that you support each other against external judgments.

2. Generational differences: partners may come from different eras and generations, leading to divergences in values, interests, and life experiences. To overcome these differences, it's essential to be open-minded and mutually understanding. Learn to appreciate the unique perspectives each brings to the relationship and find

common activities and interests that bring you closer together.

3. Expectations about the future: partners may have different expectations concerning their future, especially regarding family life, career, and personal projects. Communication is key to addressing these expectations and ensuring that you are on the same page. Be open to discussion and willing to compromise to create a fulfilling future together.

4. Health and aging challenges: age differences can also pose challenges related to health and aging. Partners may have different energy levels and health needs. It's important to show understanding and support in the face of these challenges. Be prepared to adapt to changes that occur over time and support each other through life's trials.

5. Reactions from loved ones: the reaction of family and friends can be a significant factor to consider in a relationship with an age difference. Some relatives may be hesitant or disapprove of the relationship. It's essential to address these reactions with understanding and patience while affirming your confidence in your relationship. Be prepared to explain your feelings and motivations to your loved ones and give them time to adjust to the situation.

6. Emotion management: age differences can evoke complex emotions, both among partners and those outside the relationship. Learn to manage your emotions and those of others with sensitivity and empathy. Be open to communication and emotional

expression, and ensure you create a safe and respectful space where everyone can share their feelings.

Overcoming obstacles related to age difference in a relationship requires understanding, communication, and open-mindedness. Show confidence in your relationship, support each other, and be ready to face challenges together. A fulfilling relationship is possible regardless of age difference when it's based on love, trust, and mutual understanding.

Chapter 16

Avoiding common seduction mistakes

In the process of seduction, it's easy to fall into certain common errors that can harm the budding relationship. We'll explore these common pitfalls and offer advice on how to avoid them, in order to maximize your chances of success in your seduction journey.

1. Rushing: one of the most common mistakes is rushing into seduction, wanting to move too quickly in the relationship or expressing feelings too soon. Take the time to get to know the other person, build an emotional connection, and let things develop naturally.

2. Lack of authenticity: being authentic is crucial in seduction. Avoid playing a role or pretending to be someone you're not. Be yourself and show your true personality, as that's what will truly attract the other person.

3. Lack of listening: listening to the other person is crucial in the seduction process. Don't just focus on yourself and what you have to say. Be attentive to what

the other person is saying, ask questions, and show interest in what they have to say.

4. Disregarding boundaries: it's important to respect the other person's boundaries. Don't push them to do something they don't want to or feel uncomfortable doing. Respect their choices and decisions.

5. Emotional manipulation: avoid emotionally manipulating the other person to get what you want. Be honest and sincere in your intentions and don't play with the other person's emotions.

6. Emotional dependence: it's also essential not to become too emotionally dependent on the other person early in the relationship. Maintain your independence and take care of yourself first and foremost.

7. Lack of communication: communication is the key to a successful relationship. Don't let misunderstandings accumulate by avoiding difficult conversations. Be open and honest in your exchanges with the other person.

8. Projecting expectations: avoid projecting your expectations onto the other person and trying to change them to fit your ideals. Accept them as they are and let the relationship evolve naturally.

9. Focusing on physical appearance: seduction shouldn't be limited to physical appearance. Instead, focus on personality, values, and common interests, which are more enduring elements in a relationship.

10. Impatience: patience is a virtue essential in seduction. Don't get discouraged if things don't go as planned or if the relationship doesn't develop quickly. Be patient and let time do its work.

By avoiding these common mistakes, you'll increase your chances of success in your seduction journey. Be authentic, respectful, and attentive to the other person, while maintaining your independence and communicating openly. A sincere and thoughtful approach to seduction will allow you to build strong and fulfilling relationships.

Chapter 17

Navigating the digital age and online dating

In this digital era, online dating has become a popular option to meet new people and establish connections. Navigating this virtual world can be confusing, but with the right knowledge and approaches, you can make the most of this seduction opportunity. Here's how you can master the art of online dating and leverage digital tools to capture women's attention.

1. Understanding online dating platforms: there are many online dating platforms, each with its own features and community. Understanding these different platforms will help you choose the ones that best suit your needs and goals.

2. Creating an attractive and authentic profile: your profile is your business card in the world of online dating. Learn how to create a profile that showcases you while remaining authentic, to attract women who align with your values and interests.

3. Compelling photos: photos are a crucial element of your online dating profile. Discover what type of

photos captivate women's attention and make them want to know more about you.

4. Making a compelling first contact: when approaching a woman online, the first message is crucial. Learn how to write a compelling first message that piques interest and encourages a response.

5. Effective online communication: online communication is different from face-to-face communication. Understand how to maintain engaging and interesting conversations to create a virtual connection.

6. Avoiding online dating pitfalls: online dating can be a source of disappointment if you're not careful. Learn how to avoid common pitfalls to protect yourself emotionally and make the most of this experience.

7. Planning the first in-person meeting: when you feel ready to transition from virtual communication to an in-person meeting, learn how to plan a successful and enjoyable first encounter.

8. Being captivating in the digital world: online seduction requires a different approach from seduction in person. Explore specific techniques to be captivating in the digital world and attract women to you.

By mastering the intricacies of the digital world and online dating, you can expand your opportunities to meet interesting and compatible women. The secret lies in an authentic and respectful approach, combined with a deep understanding of the digital tools at your disposal.

75

Chapter 18

Developing a mysterious and intriguing aura

In the art of seduction, cultivating a mysterious and intriguing aura can be a powerful asset. Women are often drawn to the unknown and to those who exude an air of mystery. Here's how you can develop this mysterious and intriguing aura to captivate women's attention.

1. Maintain an air of mystery: Don't reveal everything right away. Let a veil of mystery linger over certain aspects of your life. This will pique women's curiosity and prompt them to want to learn more about you.

2. Avoid divulging everything about yourself: When conversing with a woman, refrain from telling her everything about yourself right from the start. Keep some information for later, as the relationship develops.

3. Be attentive to details: Pay attention to details in your interactions with women. Show curiosity and interest in what they say, while keeping a hint of mystery about your own thoughts and emotions.

4. Use body language to intrigue: Body language can be a powerful way to communicate a mysterious aura. Use subtle gestures, intense gazes, and enigmatic smiles to intrigue and captivate women.

5. Don't rush into a relationship: Take your time to develop a relationship with a woman. Don't rush to become too intimate or too open right from the start.

6. Reveal your passions and dreams: When you feel comfortable enough with a woman, reveal your passions and dreams. This will add a mysterious dimension to your personality and demonstrate your emotional depth.

7. Avoid oversharing on social media: Social media can be a means to share your life, but avoid oversharing online. Keep some moments and aspects of your life private.

8. Cultivate a sense of adventure: Show yourself to be open to adventure and new experiences. An adventurous person is often perceived as mysterious and intriguing.

By developing a mysterious and intriguing aura, you will arouse women's interest and admiration. Remember that the goal is not to play a role, but rather to reveal different facets of your personality as the relationship progresses.

Chapter 19

Knowing how to listen and ask the right questions

One of the most important aspects of seduction is the ability to actively listen and ask the right questions. Knowing how to listen attentively demonstrates your sincere interest in the person in front of you, while asking the right questions deepens the conversation and creates a deeper connection. Here's how to develop these essential skills for successful seduction:

1. Be fully present: When you're with a woman, be fully present in the moment. Avoid distractions and focus on what she's saying.

2. Show empathy: Be empathetic towards the woman's emotions and experiences. Show that you understand and care about how she feels.

3. Ask open-ended questions: Ask open-ended questions that invite the woman to share her thoughts and feelings. Avoid closed-ended questions that only require a short answer.

4. Avoid sensitive topics: Be mindful of topics that might be sensitive for the woman and avoid addressing them insensitively.

5. Demonstrate genuine interest: Show genuine interest in what the woman has to say. Listen actively and ask follow-up questions to deepen the conversation.

6. Avoid monopolizing the conversation: Leave enough room for the woman to express herself and avoid monopolizing the conversation.

7. Consider the unsaid: Be attentive to non-verbal cues and implications. Sometimes, what's left unsaid is just as important as what's said.

8. Avoid judgment: Refrain from making hasty judgments about what the woman shares with you. Be open and respectful of her perspective.

9. Be patient and attentive: Be patient and attentive to the nuances of the conversation. Don't rush things and let the relationship develop naturally.

10. Show your sincerity: Demonstrate your sincerity towards the woman and your honest intentions in the relationship.

By developing your ability to actively listen and ask the right questions, you'll be able to create meaningful connections with the women you're seducing. Attentive listening and open communication are key to establishing authentic and lasting bonds with women, and will enable you to develop fulfilling and enriching relationships.

Chapter 20

Using body language to create attraction

Body language plays an essential role in seduction. It enables the transmission of powerful messages and creates a subtle yet potent attraction towards a woman. Here's how to effectively use body language to create attraction:

1. Maintain a confident posture: a straight and confident posture is crucial for projecting a positive image of yourself. Stand tall with shoulders slightly back, and avoid slouching or hunching.

2. Establish eye contact: eye contact is a powerful way to create a connection with a woman. Look at her eyes respectfully and warmly, but avoid staring in an intimidating manner.

3. Smile naturally: a warm and genuine smile can create a positive and welcoming atmosphere. Smile naturally when interacting with a woman.

4. Use open gestures: employ open and relaxed gestures to express your interest and openness. Avoid

closed or nervous gestures that may convey a negative impression.

5. Stand close to her: when speaking to a woman, stand at a comfortable distance but close enough to create an intimate connection.

6. Use subtle touch: subtle touches, like a light touch on the arm, can be a powerful way to create a physical connection with a woman. Be mindful of her reactions and ensure the touch is welcome.

7. Adopt a calm pace: a calm and relaxed pace in your movements and gestures can convey confidence and self-assurance.

8. Adapt your body language to the situation: be aware of the environment and situation you're in, and adapt your body language accordingly.

9. Avoid nervous gestures: steer clear of nervous or fidgety gestures that may betray your anxiety. Stay calm and composed.

10. Be attentive to her body language: pay attention to the body language of the woman you're seducing. Her gestures, facial expressions, and body language convey a lot about her feelings and interest.

By consciously and masterfully using body language, you'll be able to create a powerful and subtle attraction towards the women you're seducing. Confident, open, and positive body language can help

you establish a deeper connection and spark the interest
of the woman you desire to seduce.

Chapter 21

Developing emotional and physical intimacy

Emotional and physical intimacy is a crucial element of any fulfilling relationship. It is what allows for the creation of a deep and meaningful bond with a woman. Here's how to develop this intimacy in a healthy and respectful manner:

1. Active listening: emotional intimacy begins with active and attentive listening. Be present when you engage with your partner, listen to her thoughts, feelings, and concerns.

2. Share your emotions: to develop emotional intimacy, it's important to be open and vulnerable by sharing your emotions and feelings with your partner. This strengthens the connection and creates a space of mutual trust.

3. Express your affection: regularly expressing affection is an important way to develop physical intimacy. Show your partner that you care about her by giving compliments, offering hugs, and showing gestures of affection.

4. Foster open communication: open and honest communication is essential for developing emotional and physical intimacy. Encourage your partner to express her needs and desires, and also be open to sharing yours.

5. Respect each other's boundaries: emotional and physical intimacy requires respecting each other's boundaries. Be attentive to your partner's signals and respect her choices and needs.

6. Create moments of intimacy: take the time to create special moments of intimacy with your partner. Whether it's a romantic evening, a getaway for two, or simply a relaxing moment together, these moments will strengthen your connection.

7. Be attentive: being attentive to your partner is a powerful way to develop emotional and physical intimacy. Show her that you care by being present in important moments of her life.

8. Explore sensuality: sensuality is an important aspect of physical intimacy. Take the time to explore your sensuality together and discover what you both enjoy.

9. Foster mutual trust: mutual trust is a cornerstone of emotional and physical intimacy. Be reliable and honest in your words and actions to strengthen this trust.

10. Maintain passion: to sustain lasting emotional and physical intimacy, nurture passion in your

relationship. Keep the spark alive by being creative in your intimate moments and cultivating a deep emotional connection.

By developing healthy emotional and physical intimacy, you will create a fulfilling and balanced relationship with your partner. Be attentive to her needs, respect her boundaries, and cultivate a deep and meaningful connection that nourishes your relationship over time.

Chapter 22

Creating memorable memories together

The memories you create together play a vital role in strengthening your relationship and maintaining emotional connection. Here's how to create memorable moments that will bring you closer:

1. Plan special activities: take the time to plan special activities you can do together. Whether it's a weekend getaway, an adventurous day out, or simply a romantic dinner, these special moments will strengthen your bonds.

2. Break out of your routine: breaking the daily routine is essential for creating memorable memories. Try new activities, explore new places, and step out of your comfort zone to experience enriching moments together.

3. Capture the moments: take the time to capture your special moments by taking photos or keeping tangible mementos. These small material things will remind you of the precious moments you shared.

4. Share common passions: find common passions you can explore together. It could be a hobby, a sport, or an artistic activity. Sharing common interests strengthens your connection.

5. Celebrate important moments: don't forget to celebrate important moments in your relationship, whether it's your anniversary, valentine's day, or other significant dates. Create special traditions to make these occasions even more memorable.

6. Take risks together: dare to step out of your comfort zone by taking risks together. Whether it's traveling to an unknown country, trying a new daring activity, or facing a challenge together, these experiences will strengthen your bond.

7. Be spontaneous: spontaneity can add a magical touch to your relationship. Surprise your partner with unexpected gestures or small attentions that will create memorable memories.

8. Relive your memories: take the time to relive your memories together. Share your favorite moments, look at photos or videos, and let these memories bring you closer together.

9. Create special rituals: establish special rituals in your relationship, such as a weekly movie night, a monthly picnic, or an annual getaway. These rituals will strengthen your bond and create unique memories.

10. Focus on the emotional experience: when creating memories together, focus on the emotional

experience rather than material details. It's the shared feelings that make memories memorable.

By creating memorable memories together, you will strengthen your emotional bond and nurture your relationship in a meaningful way. Be intentional in your activities, share special moments, and cultivate a relationship filled with precious moments.

Chapter 23

Handling disputes and disagreements with maturity

In any relationship, it's normal to have disagreements and disputes. What matters most is how you handle them together. Here are some tips for managing conflicts with maturity and strengthening your relationship:

1. Active listening: When you disagree, take the time to actively listen to your partner. Show empathy and try to understand their perspective without interrupting.

2. Expressing your feelings constructively: When expressing your feelings, do so constructively and respectfully. Avoid personal attacks and focus on the specific issues you want to resolve.

3. Finding solutions together: Instead of seeking to 'win' an argument, work together to find solutions that work for both parties. Be open to compromise and finding common ground.

4. Taking a step back before reacting: When emotions are running high, take a step back before

reacting. Take a moment to reflect on the situation and your feelings before responding.

5. Not letting problems escalate: Don't ignore problems and let them escalate. Address them as soon as they arise to prevent them from escalating.

6. Respecting each other's boundaries: If your partner needs space to think or calm down, respect their boundaries. Give them the necessary time before resuming the discussion.

7. Avoiding blaming each other: Avoid blaming your partner or feeling constantly accused. Take responsibility for conflicts and seek solutions together.

8. Showing empathy: Be empathetic towards your partner and try to see things from their perspective. Understanding their feelings can help defuse conflicts.

9. Communicating openly and honestly: Open and honest communication is essential for resolving disagreements. Be transparent about your feelings and needs.

10. Learning from each disagreement: Every disagreement can be an opportunity to learn and grow as a couple. Reflect and draw lessons from each situation.

By managing differences and disagreements maturely, you'll strengthen the trust and stability of your relationship. How you approach conflicts can make the difference between a fulfilling relationship and a tense one. Be open to communication, seek solutions together, and show mutual understanding to build a lasting and fulfilling relationship.

Chapter 24

Overcoming the challenges of distance and time

In romantic relationships, challenges of distance and time can sometimes arise, especially in a modern world where jobs and responsibilities can separate us from our partners. Here are some tips for overcoming these challenges and maintaining a strong relationship despite distance and time constraints:

1. Regular communication: Maintaining regular communication is crucial when you're apart from each other. Use all means of communication at your disposal, such as phone calls, text messages, video calls, emails, and social media to connect as often as possible.

2. Setting goals and expectations: Discuss together your personal goals and what you expect from the relationship. Set realistic expectations regarding communication and time spent together to avoid disappointments.

3. Planning regular visits: If distance is a factor, plan regular visits to physically reunite. These moments

together strengthen the emotional bond and create precious memories.

4. Using technology to your advantage: Technology can be a valuable ally in overcoming distance. Share photos, videos, and moments from your daily life to feel closer to each other.

5. Managing time zone differences: If you're in different time zones, take this difference into account in your communication and visits. Find times that work for both of you to talk live.

6. Cultivating trust: Trust is the key to a successful long-distance relationship. Be honest and transparent with each other to establish a solid foundation of trust.

7. Avoiding misunderstandings: In a long-distance relationship, it's easy to misinterpret each other's messages or intentions. Clarify things if you have doubts to avoid misunderstandings.

8. Finding common activities from afar: Find activities you can do together even from a distance, such as watching a movie simultaneously, playing online games, or sharing music playlists.

9. Supporting personal goals: Encourage each other in your personal and professional goals, even if they involve spending time apart.

10. Looking towards the future: Keep in mind that the distance situation may be temporary and project

yourselves into the future, when you may be together more regularly.

By being patient, understanding, and making efforts to maintain regular communication, you can overcome the challenges of distance and time in your relationship. The key is to remain committed to each other and to cultivate love and connection, even when you're physically apart.

Chapter 25

Preparing for a committed and serious relationship

Preparing for a serious and committed relationship requires emotional, mental, and social readiness. A lasting relationship demands personal investment and a willingness to commit. Here are some tips to prepare yourself for a serious relationship:

1. Reflect on your goals and values: Before committing to a serious relationship, take the time to reflect on your personal goals and values. Ensure that you are ready to share your life with someone else and that your goals are aligned.

2. Take time to heal: If you're coming out of a past relationship, give yourself time to heal emotionally before entering into a new serious relationship. Take time to rediscover and realign yourself.

3. Be open to communication: Communication is a fundamental pillar of a serious relationship. Be open to expressing your feelings, needs, and expectations, and be willing to listen to your partner empathetically.

4. Be ready to compromise: In a serious relationship, compromises are inevitable. Be prepared to make adjustments and find solutions together when disagreements arise.

5. Know yourself: Self-awareness is crucial in a serious relationship. Identify your strengths and weaknesses, your limits, and desires, to better understand yourself and express yourself clearly.

6. Be ready to commit: Commitment is a key aspect of a serious relationship. Be prepared to commit emotionally and make plans for the future together.

7. Be honest with yourself: Be honest with yourself about your intentions in the relationship. Ensure that you're ready to commit seriously and not play with your partner's feelings.

8. Have a positive outlook on the future: A positive attitude towards the future is essential in a serious relationship. Have confidence in yourself and your partner, and approach the future with optimism.

9. Avoid external pressures: Don't let external pressures, such as family or societal expectations, influence your decision to commit to a serious relationship. Take your time to make the right decision for yourself.

10. Develop self-love: Love and respect yourself. A serious relationship requires that you love and value yourself as an individual.

Preparing for a serious relationship takes time and reflection. Take the time to know yourself, heal if necessary, and be open to communication and commitment. When you're ready, you'll be able to fully engage in a serious and fulfilling relationship with your partner.

Chapter 26

Building rapport and camaraderie

Developing closeness and camaraderie are essential elements in building a strong and fulfilling relationship. Let's explore how to develop a deep and lasting connection with your partner by cultivating closeness and camaraderie:

1. Sharing common activities: Finding activities that you both enjoy and sharing them will strengthen your emotional bond. Whether it's a passion for travel, cooking, sports, or the arts, sharing common experiences enriches your relationship.

2. Providing support and encouragement: Being a support for your partner in their projects and aspirations is crucial. Encourage them to pursue their dreams and be there to support them through life's ups and downs.

3. Developing a shared sense of humour: Laughter and humour are powerful bonds in a relationship. Share moments of laughter and fun together, and develop a shared sense of humour that allows you to overcome difficult times with lightness.

4. Communicating with complicity: Develop a secret language or gestures that are unique to the two of you. These signs of complicity will strengthen your bond and create a unique emotional intimacy.

5. Spending quality time together: The quality of time spent together is more important than quantity. Set aside distractions and focus on your partner to create intense and meaningful moments.

6. Sharing common values and goals: Having common values and goals strengthens the sense of closeness and camaraderie. Share your fundamental beliefs and work together to achieve shared goals.

7. Overcoming challenges together: Face life's challenges as a team. Whether it's financial difficulties, family problems, or important decisions, solidarity will strengthen your relationship.

8. Respecting each other's individuality: Even though you share a deep bond, it's essential to respect your partner's individuality. Give them the space to grow as an individual while cultivating your emotional connection.

9. Surprising and reigniting the flame: Surprise your partner with romantic gestures and unexpected attentions. Regularly reignite the flame of your relationship by creating special moments and showing your love unexpectedly.

10. Expressing gratitude: Regularly show gratitude to your partner for what they bring to your life. Express your appreciation and love to nurture closeness and camaraderie in your relationship.

Developing closeness and camaraderie is an ongoing process that requires constant attention and commitment. By investing in these aspects of your relationship, you will create a deep and lasting connection with your partner, thereby strengthening the solid foundation of your relationship.

Chapter 27

Maintaining passion and excitement in the relationship

Maintaining passion and excitement are key elements in keeping a relationship vibrant and fulfilling. Let's explore how to cultivate and nurture these feelings throughout your relationship:

1. Cultivate physical intimacy: Fulfilling physical intimacy is essential to keeping passion alive in a relationship. Take time to connect physically with your partner, creating intimate and romantic moments.

2. Surprise and innovate: Routine can dampen passion, so regularly surprise your partner with new ideas and unexpected experiences. Innovate in your dates, getaways, or activities to maintain excitement in the relationship.

3. Open up to new experiences: Explore new experiences together, whether it's travel, hobbies, or cultural discoveries. These new experiences stimulate excitement and strengthen your emotional bond.

4. Maintain erotic communication: Erotic communication is a way to reignite passion in the relationship. Express your desires and fantasies openly to your partner to enhance intimacy and connection.

5. Practice erotic gratitude: Express gratitude and appreciation to your partner for their sensuality and physical appeal. Offer sincere compliments to maintain self-esteem and mutual confidence.

6. Maintain mystery: Keep an element of mystery in your relationship by avoiding revealing everything to your partner. This maintains a certain level of excitement and curiosity in the relationship.

7. Dedicate quality time: Allocate quality time without distractions to nurture emotional connection and passion between you.

8. Explore sensuality: Discover sensuality in all its forms, whether through massages, caresses, or intimate moments of sharing.

9. Take care of appearance: Taking care of your physical appearance for yourself and your partner is a way to maintain attraction and passion in the relationship.

10. Develop erotic complicity: Build erotic complicity with your partner by openly communicating about your desires and needs, and by exploring your fantasies and preferences together.

Maintaining passion and excitement in a relationship requires mutual effort and openness to exploration and innovation. By developing fulfilling intimacy and nurturing erotic complicity, you will create a vibrant and fulfilling relationship that brings you closer to your partner.

Chapter 28

Understanding power dynamics and equality

We'll explore the dynamics of power and equality in romantic relationships. Understanding these aspects is essential for maintaining a healthy and fulfilling relationship:

1. Equal communication: Equal communication is a fundamental pillar of a healthy relationship. It's crucial that both partners feel heard and respected in the relationship. Avoid dominating and authoritative behaviors, and prioritize open and empathetic communication.

2. Joint decision-making: Making decisions together strengthens trust and intimacy in the relationship. Involve each other in important choices concerning your shared life.

3. Fair distribution of responsibilities: A fair distribution of responsibilities allows each partner to feel valued and involved in the relationship. Share household chores and family responsibilities evenly.

4. Acceptance of differences: Every individual is unique, and it's essential to accept and respect each other's differences. Avoid trying to change your partner and learn to appreciate their uniqueness.

5. Recognition of individual needs: Recognizing and respecting each partner's individual needs is fundamental. Make sure to maintain a balance between personal needs and those of the relationship.

6. Conflict management: Learn to manage conflicts constructively, avoiding aggressive or manipulative behaviors. Seek to understand each other's viewpoints and find solutions together.

7. Autonomy and independence: It's important to preserve autonomy and independence in a relationship. Maintain your personal passions and interests while sharing moments of closeness with your partner.

8. Mutual trust: Trust is the foundation of a strong relationship. Be honest and transparent with your partner, and avoid controlling or monitoring their actions.

9. Financial equality: Financial equality contributes to establishing balance in the relationship. Share expenses and financial responsibilities fairly.

10. Expression of love and gratitude: Regularly express your love and gratitude to your partner. This will strengthen emotional connection and contribute to maintaining a fulfilling relationship.

Understanding and practicing these dynamics of power and equality will cultivate a fulfilling relationship based on mutual respect and harmony between partners. By fostering equal communication and respecting each other's needs and differences, you'll create a balanced and fulfilling relationship that brings happiness and mutual fulfillment.

Chapter 29

Making decisions for the future of the relationship

We will address the various important decisions to make for the future of your relationship. Making decisions together is essential for building a solid and fulfilling future:

1. Common goals: Discuss and determine the common goals you want to achieve as a couple. Whether it's personal, professional, or family projects, having common goals will help you build a shared vision for the future.

2. Level of commitment: Evaluate together the level of commitment you want to have in the relationship. This may include discussions about the possibility of living together, getting married, or starting a family.

3. Compromises: Be prepared to make compromises to maintain harmony and balance in the relationship. Making decisions together often means finding solutions that work for both partners.

4. Handling the unexpected: Anticipate that unforeseen events may occur in the relationship and

discuss the best way to handle them. Open communication and flexibility are essential for overcoming unexpected challenges.

5. Long-term relationship vision: Discuss your vision for the long-term relationship. This will ensure that your expectations and goals are aligned.

6. Expressing needs and desires: Don't hesitate to express your needs and desires for the future of the relationship. Honest communication is essential for building a fulfilling relationship.

7. Importance of adaptability: Be open to change and the evolution of the relationship. Life is full of changes, and it's important to be adaptable to face the different stages of the relationship.

8. Conflict resolution: Learn to resolve conflicts in a constructive and respectful manner. Disagreements may arise, but knowing how to manage them will help you maintain a strong and harmonious relationship.

9. Commitment to mutual growth: Be committed to personal and mutual growth. Encourage each other to pursue your passions and interests while supporting your individual projects.

10. Making decisions as a team: Remember that you are a team and you make decisions together for the future of your relationship. This will strengthen your emotional connection and mutual trust.

By making decisions together for the future of the relationship, you will establish a solid foundation for building a fulfilling and harmonious life. Remember that each relationship is unique, and it's important to create a common vision that meets the needs and desires of each partner. By cultivating open communication and a commitment to mutual growth, you will build a lasting and fulfilling relationship that brings you happiness and fulfillment in the long run.

Chapter 30

To thrive in successful seduction

This book has been designed to provide you with the necessary tools to develop authentic and fulfilling relationships with the women you are interested in. We will now highlight the key points you need to remember to thrive in your seduction journey:

1. Self-confidence: Self-confidence is the cornerstone of successful seduction. Build positive self-esteem by focusing on your strengths and accepting your weaknesses. Believe in yourself and your ability to attract women.

2. Authenticity: Be yourself and take pride in who you are. Women appreciate authenticity and sincerity. Avoid trying to play a role or be someone you are not.

3. Communication: Master the art of verbal and non-verbal communication. Listen actively and show interest in what women have to say. Be attentive to their signals of interest and disinterest.

4. Understanding women: Take the time to understand women's expectations and desires. Each

woman is unique, and it is important not to generalize or make assumptions based on stereotypes.

5. Listening to your needs: Remember that your needs and desires are also important in a relationship. Ensure that the relationship is mutually satisfying and fulfilling.

6. Establishing healthy boundaries: Be clear about your boundaries and do not compromise your values. A healthy relationship is based on mutual respect and consent.

7. Relationship evolution: Understand that relationships evolve and change over time. Be open to challenges and opportunities that arise, and be adaptable.

8. Passion and excitement: Maintain passion and excitement in the relationship by paying attention to your partner's needs and exploring new experiences together.

9. Making decisions as a team: Make important decisions together as a team. Communication and collaboration are essential for building a strong and harmonious future.

10. Confidence in the future: Be confident in the future of your relationship and in your ability to cultivate a fulfilling connection with your partner.

Successful seduction is based on authenticity, self-confidence, effective communication, and mutual respect. Remember that each relationship is unique, and it is important to build a relationship that meets your needs and those of your partner. Develop a relationship based on love, trust, and mutual fulfillment, and you will discover a life filled with happiness and satisfaction with the woman who suits you best.

Table of contents

By the same author

(« Seduction » series)

- The art of verbal seduction : mastering words to attract and captivate.

- Wedding speeches and congratulations : a comprehensive guide to unforgettable words.

- How to become a femme fatale: the ultimate guide to seduction.

- How to seduce a man: secrets to enchant him forever.

Orders and availability

Our publications are all available and can be ordered on Amazon. Check out Amazon to discover our new books and other series.

9 798887 970129 6